Raising Tiny Boss Babies

Doing it your way

Georgia Scheible

DISCLAIMER: The information presented in this book is intended for educational purposes only. This book is not intended to be a replacement for medical or psychological advice given by a professional. You should seek the services of a professional if you need expert advice. The publisher and author are not offering professional services advice. The publisher and author assume no responsibility for your actions and specifically disclaim responsibility for any liability, loss, risk, or any emotional, physical, or psychological damages, incurred as a consequence, directly or indirectly, of any of the contents in this book.

COPYRIGHT THE BEHAVIOR BOSS 2023: All rights reserved. No part of this publication may be reproduced, distributed, or transmitted in any form, without prior written permission of the publisher. For permission requests, email info@thebehaviorboss.com.

The Behavior Boss

www.thebehaviorboss.com

Raising Tiny Boss Babies: Doing it your way- 1st ed.

I dedicate this book to my loving husband, Joseph, and my children, Alexa, Abigail, and Ashlinn.

The ones who believed in me. Who kept pushing me to show up. You are the foundation of all I am and all I do.

Introduction

Thinking back to how I did the whole parenting thing with my first child I realized that there were so many things that I did because I thought I needed to. Because of pressure from society, family, friends, the internet, influencers and anybody who was a nobody. I was engulfed in this parenting world that didn't feel like me. A world that felt like it was slowly taking me under and made me second guess if I was doing anything right raising my sweet baby.

I remember comparing myself to other moms and thinking I was not doing enough. Thinking that if I didn't do all the things, I somehow was less than.

You see, even being well-educated, in psychology none the less and having spent a good portion of my life working with children I still bought into the bullshit.

This one summer day was the day that changed it all for me. I had just passed my licensing boards and I was working on my next project that later would become my own private practice treating children. I was so busy with two littles and trying to get a practice started that I had little time to myself. This specific day I was sitting in my living room in Marina Del Rey, CA with my oldest daughter and her new baby sister. The baby was sleeping soundly in her bassinet and her sister was looking at books in the cozy corner. I had a few moments of silence and I was scrolling through my phone on

Instagram looking at all these pages. This is something I often did so that wasn't anything out of the ordinary. Except for this day, something was eating at me. Something did not sit well. I had these immense feelings towards these Instagram pages and pictures. I was triggered by them. The baby woke up and I got distracted with mom duty.

Later that evening, when everyone was asleep and I was lying in bed I remember trying to understand why I was so triggered. What had bothered me so much. And then it clicked. That was the day that I told myself I would no longer succumb to all this nonsense. The day that I decided that I was going to do what I knew as a parent needed to be done to raise my children.

That I didn't need any "specialist" or influencer to tell me how I was going to parent.

You see, society has a way of sneaking it's influence on you. You have to be stronger than that. You have to rise above it all. You get to choose what you want for your life, for your family, for your children. It can look whatever way feels good and right to you.

As I made this intentional choice to start raising my children the way I wanted to and saw fit, I also made a promise. That promise was that I was going to change this notion and rhetoric that we have around parenthood and empower parents to make choices and decisions for their families that fit with their beliefs. This was the moment of clarity for me and the guidance that set up the foundation of my private practice.

I knew when I started out that I was going to be going against the grain. But I was up for the challenge. I knew that there would be people who would question or might not be ready to accept what I was saying. And that was ok. I wasn't looking for approval or acceptance. The only thing I wanted was to create a space where, parents and children could be seen and heard without judgment. A place where each family could function in a way that served them best. A world where we didn't have so much confusion on parenting strategies.

So, over the years I built my practice, I treated thousands of parents and children, I spoke at many engagements, I presented teacher workshops at several private schools in the Los Angeles area, I created a parenting course, hosted several parent workshops, and opened a new business The Behavior Boss.

The Behavior Boss became my new baby. You see, there's a clinical space where I as an expert give clinical advice to treat and there's a space where I wanted to be able to freely talk about parenting and children that didn't involve clinical expertise. So, a new branch sprouted and The Behavior Boss has been the foundation of Parenting with Intention.

And now I have you, who has picked up this book for a reason. Maybe you have been feeling overwhelmed with all the parenting stuff also. Maybe you are confused with all the parenting theories and strategies telling you how to effectively raise your child. Maybe you have children and are now realizing that the different parenting approaches you have been using are not working for you.

Whatever the reason is that brought you to my book, Welcome.

Welcome to a place where you can pick and choose what works for you and what aligns with you. A place where you will not be judged or told that you have to do something a certain way to get some result. A place where things will be real and raw.

I am here with you and will help guide you to a place of clarity when it comes to how you parent. I will help you do the work so you can become clear on what you want for you, your child, your family.

Everything I say comes from a place of true passion. A place of comfort. It will be real at times. I don't sugar coat anything and I certainly don't follow the majority or the "experts". If it speaks to you great. If it doesn't that's fine too. Take what you want and apply it in the way that it works for you.

We have to stop the madness that is being sold to us about how to raise children. Even more, we need to get back to the basics because we are raising a generation of children who will become self entitled brats. They are going to drown in the real world because when they are faced with reality, they will not be able to cope.

I invite you to read the chapters and take what speaks to your soul. Feel free to re-read sections as needed. Apply it to your life and your parenting journey as you see fit.

I want to leave you with one thing. Believe in yourself. Trust that you were meant to be a parent and that you always have the best intentions for your child. You know your child best and don't let anyone else tell you otherwise. Create the environment that you feel is right for your child. You can do it all in the way you want. Period.

Reminiscing

I remember as a little girl dreaming of becoming a mommy. There was no other job for me as my 5-year-old self.

This was a part of all my fantasy dreams and play. I spent my days dreaming of what I thought in my growing brain "mommy-hood" would be like.

I have vivid memories in my childhood home playing with my sister but one that stands out was what we called "house". I would take my dolls in the bathroom, which was dubbed my "home", and shut the door. I would set up shop in the bathtub making beds for my babies, feeding them toothpaste soup, playing with them and waiting for my sister, whose house was the other bathroom in our home, to come over.

Knock knock....

"I'm coming" I'd say as I ran to the door.

In would come my sister with her babies for a visit.

We would play "house" for hours. We would take our babies and go shopping in our store that was filled with all sorts of toys. We would make dinner for them and give them baths and put them to bed.

I was lucky enough to have a sister and we played like this for endless hours each day. Those were the days. The days I wish that all little girls get to experience.

Oh, to be a child again.

Aren't these what childhood girl days consisted of for every little girl?

These childhood memories manifested into reality when I had my own children. Which let me tell you was a journey on its own. Leaving that for another book.

Since life had other plans for me and I struggled with infertility, I went to school and kept going to earn higher degrees to keep my mind off of the fact that I wasn't able to get pregnant. Before I knew it, I was gaining my clinical experience and preparing to get licensed as a child therapist.

Bam. I find out I'm pregnant. It was the best day of my life. My dreams were coming true. I began having flashbacks to childhood and reminiscing what I envisioned mom life was going to be like.

I thought everything was going to be perfect.

That I would have angel babies. I mean, I was a child therapist. I had all the training on managing behaviors in children. Why would I expect anything different with my own children. I got this. It's simple.

What was I thinking?

What world was I living in?

Fast forward 27 years later when I gave birth to my first child, Alexa, and I became a Mommy to a tiny human bundle of joy.

Don't get me wrong, she filled my heart with so much love. A love I never knew before.

But……and I say this from a place of love……

Man did this whole being a mommy throw me in for a ride.

The post-partum depression hit hard. I was up nursing all night long. I forgot what sleep even was. I felt alone.

All the things nobody talks about.

Slowly, things got better. We had routines. Those helped tremendously. My old friend, sleep, made her way back into my life.

I thought "Hey, I can do this" and that I did!

It was a journey for her and I. A journey we were figuring out together. One day at a time.

I wish I knew then what I know now. Maybe things would have been different. I keep thinking if I was prepared and knew more then maybe I wouldn't have had postpartum anxiety. But the reality is we are never fully prepared. What I had was a lot of patience.

Patience was key. I was patient with myself and patient with my little girl. This is what saw us through.

As a first-time mom I wanted to do all the things. Not because society was telling me to, but because I truly enjoyed it. We had the big first birthday party, we did the holiday cards, the monthly baby pictures and bought all the toys imaginable. We had all the baby gadgets. We lived life the way we wanted to and to its fullest.

Then I was crazy enough to do it all over again.

Here I found myself with a two-year-old and another on the way. I didn't know what to expect. This was uncharted territory. What I did know was that I could do it. That I would give it my all.

I enjoyed life as a family of 3 and lived each day with one goal. Raising a happy confident child. Alexa was a force all on her own. She challenged me in ways I never knew I could be challenged. I embraced it. I let her be her.

It made me stronger. It made our relationship more vibrant. The entire time all I could think was "she's a mini copy of me".

When Abigail made her debut, life changed. Yes, there was more involved with taking care of two littles. Yes, I was tired. Yes, there were times where I was so exhausted, I didn't know if I would make it another day.

I was struck again this time with postpartum anxiety. It kicked my butt. It took me to places I never wish to go back to.

But I survived.

I survived because I made the conscious decision that I would enjoy every moment I was given with these girls.

I remember one day watching out the window as the girls were dancing around and laughing thinking to myself, I could do this again.

It didn't feel daunting this time around. Maybe because I had been around the rodeo twice now.

Maybe because I had the mentality that I was already in it so what would another possibly do to shake up my world.

Social media had taken over the world and I remember sitting in bed pumping and scrolling.

Those late night and early morning feedings when nobody was awake but me. I felt myself becoming consumed with all the beautiful Instagram pages of moms and their lives. Looking at all these put together families. All these moms with perfect Instagram children on magical vacations. The anxiety grew for me. The thought that I needed to live up to some expectation was creeping in slowly. The thought that maybe I wasn't doing enough.

It consumed me.

I bought into all the bullshit with taking these cute monthly photos, having these elaborate birthday celebrations, cooking these expansive meals, shopping for all the adorable clothes and shoes. The list goes on. What was different this time was that I really didn't want to do it. I was doing it because I felt if I didn't, I was not doing my job as a mom and was somehow failing my children.

I was drowning this time because it was double the work now. I struggled because it was something I enjoyed doing before yet it never felt like enough and now, I was outnumbered and time was not on my side.

But on the outside the world saw a happy, put together, over the top mama.

I enjoyed this season of my life don't get me wrong. My dream of being a mama many times over was well on its way to fruition. And for that I was grateful.

I was a stay-at-home mama and my life was beautiful. That I will not discredit.

Ooops. Here I go again. I woke up one morning not feeling 100. I chalked it up to possibly another cold since those were pretty common with two littles around.

After a couple days I knew something wasn't right when aunt flo didn't make her appearance.

I headed straight to the store and bought the trusted old test. Came home and tested. Low and behold two lines. Pregnant.

Was this really happening?

Now, two toddlers and the third is about to make her way into my world.

How was I going to manage this?

Something shifted for me. The universe was telling me something. I began telling myself that there was no expectation of me. That I didn't have to do what others were doing or what "experts" were telling me to do.

Wait. I was an "expert" myself. Why did I feel like I had to listen to another "experts" on how to raise my children?

I could raise my children the way I saw fit. In a way that worked for my family. If I wanted to take the pictures I would. If I wanted the elaborate party, I could. If I wanted to move my baby into her room at 2 months, I could. Store bought baby food could be an option. Formula was acceptable. Screen time was up to me.

It was all possible if it's what I wanted. And if I didn't then I was allowing myself the pass. When I was clear with myself and ready to let go of all the bullshit with how to parent there was a weight lifted off my shoulders.

We prepared for another little human to join our circus.

Ashlinn made her way into our world and now here I was with 3 littles.

3 little boss babies.

Life was chaotic at times.

Life was different.

Life was beautiful.

Yes, I was on the no sleep team and I felt like my body belonged to someone else.

I had someone attached to my leg, someone on my hip and someone on my boob all the time.

But I loved it. Every minute of it.

I loved being needed so much.

It took time to figure out my new role. My new life.

Who I was.

But I never had any expectations. I just let things come as they did and I dealt with things as I felt compelled to deal with them.

It was glorious.

Freedom at its finest.

Not having to research and read and buy the books was empowering. I was meant for this and I knew what my family needed more than anyone else.

Ashlinn was the easiest baby of all 3 of them. Easiest maybe because I had been around the block twice before or maybe I felt like I knew what I was in for this time. I'm sure that helped my sanity. But I was also a different parent. I had intentionally made a choice to parent differently this time around.

And all 3 of my children benefited.

I stopped reading the books. Stopped googling at all hours of the night on how to parent.

I went with my gut. I knew enough about parenting and could apply what felt right for our family.

This was the key. What felt right for our family.

Life was great. I had never felt better. My children were all happy. They were thriving and growing into tiny boss babies.

This was the vibe I had dreamed of. And I was living it. I was doing it my way.

I wish I hadn't lost those early years to my internal identity crisis of trying to figure out who I was now that I had children.

I wish someone had told me.

Maybe they did and I wasn't listening. Likely because I was so worried about doing it right. Or maybe I was sleep deprived and only heard bits and pieces.

But you can listen.

Your children don't define who you are. Your children love you unconditionally. Live the life you want the way you want. Raise them to be happy, contributing members of society. Raise them to be independent and confident.

Whatever that looks like for your family.

Journal Prompt Break

I want you to take some time before you move through the book and reflect on some things.

- I want you to think about your journey so far. What has it been like for you?

- Think about how you parent. Has it been working for you? Why or why not.
- What do you want your child to remember most about their childhood?
- What wishes and hopes do you have for your child?
- What is your ultimate parenting goal?
- What habits do you have that you don't want your child to pick up? What is your plan for dropping those habits?
- Name one thing that you feel is keeping you from being the best parent that you can be to your child. How can you change it?

Figuring it out

One mom and three little girls trying to take on the whole big world one day at a time.

Nothing to sugar coat.

There were days where I was buried deep and it felt like there were not enough hours in a day or not enough of me to get everything done.

The first go around I wanted everything perfect.

I wanted to have a clean house, the dishes done nightly, laundry daily, a hot meal for dinner and a shower each day. By the time the second rolled around I knew this was not going to be sustainable. I let a lot of things slide and lowered my expectations.

It was either that or my sanity.

Then the third baby boss made an entrance and it was a zoo at our house. Literally.

3 baby boss girls and a husband. I had to quickly make some adjustments in life.

I decided that I was going to have zero expectations.

Whatever I accomplished that day would be good enough.

And some days I just stayed in my pj's and played all day.

My only priority was keeping the littles alive.

There were periods of post-partum depression and anxiety.

I attribute a lot of that to the unrealistic expectations I had about being a mom and trying to work through them and get to a place that felt right.

Stop the madness now for your sanity. Listen, the perfect life as a mom does not exist. It's only perfect if it works for you.

Kids need a lot of things. This is the truth. It can be tiring. Overwhelming. They require a lot of our attention.

Even when we have no more to give, they are right there wanting more.

Life is different with kids. When I understood that life would just be different, it became more joyful for me.

Patience was one thing I learned early on. Having worked with kids most of my life, I knew patience was a must.

Get on board with this now.

If you can learn to have patience, or at least work at it you will be happier. Your children will be happier. Remind yourself often that children are learning. They are watching your every move to see how you handle things. If you don't have patience they won't either. Be patient with yourself and with them. Everyone is learning and adjusting.

Patience is hard. It's hard when you're expected to do the extraordinary, all day every day. When you are being pulled in every direction and stretched so thin yet you still have to keep going.

You'll lose your shit some days. That's OK. Just pick yourself up, take a moment and collect and keep moving forward. Work at it. Take those deep breaths when you're feeling overwhelmed.

Letting you in on a little secret. Children do not wake up in the morning thinking about how they can make your life hell today. They just don't. They wake up ready for a new day and some days bring on more challenges for them and they need your guidance to get through it. Their behaviors and actions are just that. Nothing else. Behaviors and actions. If we can learn to not take things personally as parents and just realize that our kids need us for something that they are struggling with then we can parent from a very different perspective. This allows us the opportunity to help them without our emotions getting in the way.

Trips, dinners out, shopping, cooking, cleaning, family gatherings, holidays are all different.

Different. Not bad. Just different. The quicker you get on board with this mentality the better your family life with children will be.

But it gets easier.

The life you're living that is.

Children don't get easier you just get stronger. Better at doing what you do.

They mature.

You learn.

Once upon a time I held on to the words "this too shall pass".

I mean it felt like every person who saw me with all 3 kids in tow would smile and say these words.

I legit thought there was some magical time when being a mom became easy. As my children grew out of the baby phase, I realized this doesn't exist. There is no easier, it's just a different phase.

Instead of waiting for things to "get easier", I accepted all the tantrums, talking back, messes, and middle of the night bed takeovers.

It's where I was meant to be at the time.

Figuring out how to raise my babies was something that never was concrete and written in stone.

I allowed it to be fluid.

To change based on their personalities and needs.

What worked for one child did not mean that it would for the next. I knew each of my children were different. They required different parenting strategies.

The explaining and talking it through worked for one. The other didn't want an explanation. She just wanted the solution and some space. I learned and got to know what they each needed from me. I worked on being the parent that they each needed. It's OK if it looks different for each child.

Whoa, it was a lot sometimes. I had to take those deep breaths. Take the walks. Tell them that I need my space right now.

I accepted that not everything will go according to plan and was always ready to adapt.

This is a must.

Kids have a mind of their own and they don't always understand that we have something planned out. They always have perfect timing to have those epic moments. Or when they decide that right before you're leaving for that party is a great time for them to have that epic blow out. Now you have to stop and change them and clean this huge mess. You're late to the party. You're flustered. But guess what? You can continue in your pitty party or you can decide to be positive. It can be a big deal or it can be just something you have to deal with. You get to decide.

Make your life easier. Take care of the situation and move on.

Remember that you are the model for your child. Everyday everything you do your child is watching. They watch how you treat others, when you offer to help someone, when you hold the door behind you and the list goes on. Children learn by observing and then modeling the behavior they see. So, start here. Model for them what it is you want to see from them. Raising socially-emotionally connected children is the goal.

Raising 3 littles has made me grow more than anything else I have done in my life.

The best part, I did it how I wanted to do it.

Yes, I read books, I followed the instagramers and watched all the TikTok's. Like I said before, it's all at our fingertips these days. So, it's hard to ignore.

When I got to the place where I did not allow myself to take any one single piece of advice from anything or anyone, that's when it all changed.

I took the information and decided how it would work for my family.

It wasn't easy.

I decided I was not going to allow outside influence to dictate how I would raise my children.

This I held on to dearly, even now. Because I'm in it.

Deep.

They need me for so much right now. Even though it can be crazy, insanely loud, exhausting, I can like it. I've waited my whole life for these babies. So I welcome the loud, messy, insanely chaotic life we have.

This is what I've realized, parents of littles need some straightforward permission to do or be or have.

So here it is.

I am giving it to you.

You can be exhausted.

You're up all hours of the night as the world sleeps tending to 3 million drinks of water, nursing, putting covers back on cold little bodies, telling the monster in the closet to leave your house, planning dinners, doing homework or packing lunches.

You can be happy.

You are raising little version of you. You're getting to live through these little loves all over again. The way they look at you, the smiles, the unsolicited "I love you" that shatters your heart into a million pieces.

You can take time for yourself.

And you should.

Daily.

Even if that's a bubble bath at night when they are in bed. You need to have your space for even a few moments each day.

It's all legit. It's all good. It's all OK. And it still can equal tired. So be it.

You can live life.

Live it with them.

We can be OK with slowing down, taking a moment and savoring the view. We can be OK with being a few minutes late. We can be OK with saying "No" to some things so that we can say "yes" to what matters most.

There are different seasons in parenthood. Some consume you. Some give you more time. Some are hard. Some are hard to say bye to. Some test you. Some help you grow. Some make you feel like you're losing you.

Parenthood is full of seasons and not all seasons look the same for everyone.

Stop the comparing.

It can be easy to fall into that trap that the world has set up. I've been guilty of comparing to others. I would think "how can she manage all the things and I'm over here drowning?". I quickly re-frame the thought in my head. I will manage what I can in the best way that I can.

The comparing game has created a world where shame, ignorance and jealousy have taken over.

Children want one thing.

Your love and attention. Period. Nothing else.

Stop caring about what others are doing or what they will think. None of that matters. There will always be those haters. Get them out of your circle. Quickly.

The holidays have a way of magnifying the comparison trap. You know what I'm talking about. All the pretty greeting cards that show up in our mailbox. The outings doing all the holiday things. The decorated homes.

Guess what? Stop that bullshit.

Focus on your holiday magic.

You don't have to do the matching outfits, the magical outings, the activities, or the cute photos.

If this isn't your vibe then don't do it. You are still a great parent. If it is your vibe, then good for you. Keep on doing it.

Every house has a mess somewhere, a crying little human, and hard moments amidst the magic. The pictures you see are just the highlights. Not the whole picture. So don't compare.

Just knowing they are all seasons helps.

Some days you'll rock parenting and some days parenting will rock you.

That's OK.

Let's shift our focus. Parenting has a way of allowing resentment in. The mental load can be overwhelming, there are not enough hours in the day, our village doesn't look the way we hoped, we don't have time for self care and we might be losing our identity. Resentment sets in. This robs you of happiness. You have to learn to talk about it, ask for help, and make things work for your family. You cannot allow these negative emotions to rob you of your happiness.

What if you spent your energy teaching your children.

Teach them what you know.

Let them get dirty.

Let them fold laundry with you.

Play hard.

Play with them every day.

This is what they really want. They don't care what other parents are doing with their kids. So why do you?

It's a disservice we do to parents, making the expectation be that everything doesn't change with parenthood. It's OK if your priorities have changed, the things that excite you have changed, and your struggles have changed. And it's also OK if it takes you some time to figure out this new you. We don't bounce back, we evolve.

The pressures from society are real. But we get to choose if we're going to allow them in.

There's a push-pull, taking time for yourself as a parent.

Being told by society to practice self-care, but being shamed when you are away from your kids.

Wanting the time to fill yourself outside of your parent role, but missing your kids when you are away.

But your time for you as the parent is important too.

We will talk more about self-care and why it has to be part of your life later.

Journal Prompt Break

I want you to stop here and take the time now to think about what you want parenting to be life for you. What feels right for you and your family.

Think about society, your village, the way you were raised. Do any of those things trigger emotions for you? Do you want to change anything?

If you are reading this book right now it's because something called your attention to it. What are you lacking or wishing to change on your parenting journey?

- What will you miss most when this season of parenthood is over? How can you savor it more today?
- What have been your favorite moments as a parent?
- What is your child's personality like? If you have multiple children, are they different or the same?

- What have you discovered about yourself since becoming a parent?
- What area do you need to improve in? Patience? Consistency? Calmness?

The Contradictions

We live in a world of great contradiction. On one hand we have unprecedented advances in technology.

We literally have all the information at our fingertips.

Yet, at the same time we are seeing an alarming escalation of children who cannot function in this world. Read that again. It is very scary what is happening to this generation of children. I will elaborate on this because it's something that must be told. You might not like hearing what I'm about to say. That's is OK. I'm going to say it anyway.

So, you just found out you're pregnant. Congratulations! Quickly run and get all the pregnancy books that will tell you how to sleep, what to eat, what to drink, what prenatal classes to take, how you should give birth and what you can expect when your little bundle of joy arrives. While you're at it, grab all the newborn books so you can learn what color poop needs to be, how many times to feed your baby and when you should move the bassinet out of your room. Your baby arrives and now you need to quickly get enrolled in a baby class so you can engage your child. Also don't forget the book on breastfeeding. You must breastfeed because that's how your baby will be a genius. If you can't produce milk that's OK then formula will have to do. While you're at it, get started on the 505 parenting books. That will be a good start.

But don't worry dozens more will be added every year.

Your zombie state now has you perplexed and wondering how you can sleep better. Hurry, there are books on this too. While you're there grab the books on sleep training your baby or not because its cruel and they will forever feel abandoned. Hold on, your baby only cries because they need your attention. So just let them cry it out. They can't have your attention all the time. Better yet, put the baby in your bed, and hope you don't accidentally smother them while they sleep, but your baby now will feel loved and a sense of attachment.

You made it through the first year!!! Donate all the baby books and move on to the toddler stage. Potty training is around the corner. Do you do the 2 day, the 5 day, the commando, never mind just let your child tell you when they are ready. Now you're wondering how do you raise your child to be successful and a functioning member of society. There are books and podcasts. Place that amazon order for new books because you really need to learn how to be present and attentive to your child but don't be that helicopter parent. Children need to learn. You can't save them every time. Set the boundaries but they have to learn from experience too. Teach them to express their feelings but only in a way that's appropriate. There are tons of books on how you can parent mindfully, the way the French do it, with positivity, no drama, and in the most unique way best suited for your child yet magically described in a book written for every child. School is approaching, yes you guessed it. Don't be too late on getting in on the action or your child will be behind. Start with the alphabet and then make sure they can count to 285 and can write their name. Don't forget they must be in 7 extracurricular activities but also keep in mind children need downtime. Screen time will damage their brains and give them tumors but download the 901 apps that will teach your child math and reading or even a new language. Yes, the more languages a child knows the smarter they are.

Are you suffocating yet? Don't worry, college isn't too far off. If you've made it this far, you're golden. There are books to make your life easier.

Or, hey, what if you didn't buy the books, listen to the people, or subscribe to any of this bullshit. There's a thought!

Here's what I think and believe deeply. There's too much out there. We have become a world with millions of theories and studies and books and podcasts. The internet is flooded with information on how to parent. This information is coming from all sorts of people but the ones that rub me the wrong way are the nobodies. You know what I am talking about. The "influencers", the parent coaches, the people that call themselves "therapists" as if they earned that title. We all of a sudden have a ton of know it all's. They preach about how to raise your child and what approach to use. We have a generation of "gentle parents" and "conscious parents" or "mindful parents" and this has all equated to no parenting.

We have gone so far off the path it's ridiculous. And let me tell you, we're going to pay for it. We are going to have a generation of children that won't be able to handle real life. A generation of children that will have a rude awakening in the real world.

Here's the thing. Many people don't even understand what gentle parenting really is. There are boundary settings with gentle parenting. There is follow through. It's not all positive language and giving your child everything they want. But people have taken it to another level and have used it as an excuse not to parent.

Gentle parenting becomes permissive parenting. Parents are second guessing their decisions. "Do I have enough boundaries?" "Do I have too few boundaries?" "Should I let this slide?" "Should I punish this behavior or should we talk it out?"

You know what I'm talking about. It's just all too much. If you do something "wrong" you risk damaging your child. This is the narrative now. The idea that somehow, we are damaging our children by doing or not doing certain things based on nonsense.

You guys. Enough. Enough with the bullshit.

The children I see walking around now are going to have the toughest time in the real world. When they have to leave their little "gentle home" and go out into the real world they will be faced with many challenges. The world is not a gentle place.

When their boss tells them that their performance is lacking or when they are given negative feedback about their performance it will sound like something they've never heard before. How do you think they will handle this? Let me tell you, they will have zero coping skills to survive in the real world. If you are parenting as a gentle parent or a conscious parent or some other form of parenting where you sweet talk to your child, and let them decide what's best, and cater to their every emotion or allow them to behave in ways that are inappropriate for a child to be behaving then you are setting our child up for failure. Unless you plan to keep them in your bubble then I suggest you take a good look at how you're parenting.

These children will grow up to be self entitled adults that behave like brats. Yes. I said it. It's already happening with all the gen z babies. They are out there looking for jobs and when they find one, they last a couple months because they can't handle the demands and rules/standards they are being held to.

I see it in my own business. I hire them, give them one piece of feedback and they quit. They can't meet the demands because they are living in a world that doesn't exist.

I am not saying that we can't be compassionate. That we can't be understanding as parents. That we shouldn't allow feelings. Yes, these are all important things. But there needs to be a balance. There needs to be parenting. Children need to learn that they won't get everything they want when they want it. That there is authority. That there are rules that later become laws. They have to experience failure. They have to learn to work through it. They have to know that things wont always go their way. We need to get back to the basics.

Wake up people. Look around. Use your brain. When you are late for work you have choices right? You can decide well I'm late so I'll talk to my boss and explain. You can decide, I'm going to speed and try to get there on time. You can decide I'm just going to call out sick. Whatever it is you get to decide. But you know there will be a consequence one way or the other for your actions. If you decide to speed you risk getting pulled over and getting a ticket. Natural consequence. We might take that chance and that's fine. Our children need to learn this fundamental thing. There are consequences in life. Some bigger than others. This is what is lacking in parenting today.

Let's take a look at attachment parenting. This theory has been one that many parents cling to as the bible on raising a child. The theory doesn't say you *can't* put your baby down. It's very clear that parents need to take care of themselves too. But when parents are in the trenches and sleep deprived, they miss the nuances. We want something absolute to cling to. The idea becomes that our baby needs our undivided attention at *all* times. We run with that.

What we are failing to see is that no one child is alike. They are all different.

How can we take one theory or one book or person preaching on how to parent seriously. You can't.

It's even worse when this person has no education or background working with children in a therapeutic environment and they are out there making claims on how to change behavior and what you should be doing with your child. Like they know your child.

And even more than that, if you get stuck on any one parenting philosophy, you won't be able to trust the person who knows your child the best: YOU.

Our parenting instincts run deep. We should listen to them.

Let's make an intentional decision to get away from this garbage.

Let's trust that we know what our child needs. Nobody knows better than you. You know what works and what simply does not. Trust yourself.

It's not that advice from others isn't useful. It can be. But parenting is never a one-size-fits-all kinda thing. Take what works for you and throw the rest in the trash where it belongs.

Do you want to know the biggest parenting secret?

The secret is that no one really knows what they are doing.

It can feel like some parents have their shit together more so than others.

For me it's the moms at school pick up who have their makeup and hair done, Starbucks in hand and appear collected all the time.

I'm just trying to pick up my kids and get home. I'm not trying to impress anyone at the pickup line. And that's OK. It's all OK. Whatever vibe you pick.

Today, I live life how I want to live it. In the way that works for my family.

It's available for you too.

There is no script.

Whatever you want to do and how you want to do it is great.

Tell yourself that on repeat.

Remember, you are the expert on your child and your family.

You do you.

Sure, there are ways to manage behavior that are backed by years of research and studies and they are effective but even then, you have to take it and make it work for your child and your family.

I have nothing against licensed professionals speaking about these topics. I included. What sends me on a tail spin is the so called "experts" and their public display of "knowledge". These people don't work with children in a clinical setting, they don't treat children or families. Their "information" if you can even call it that is based on their perception and maybe their parenting of their own child. That's it. Why are parents so fascinated by these people? Let me tell you, because when we are in the trenches and are desperate for any help or advice, we latch on to what sounds good. But the reality is that it's not the same for every child or parent or family. More importantly, why do we feel the need to do what others are doing? Why can't we use our own brains, our own intuition, our own beliefs and parent how we feel is most appropriate for our child? We can. You can. I give you permission to parent the way you want to parent. With your values and ethics that you want to instill in your child. Of course we all want our children to be happy. We want to be gentle. We want to respect them. When we read some of this garbage, we get in the mindset that this is the only thing we have to do. What we are missing now more than ever is the boundaries. The rules. The parental authority. It has been pushed to the side and all the power has been given to the child. This is a huge mistake.What we have now is a world where parents are more confused than ever.

With all these parenting theories and books and podcasts we have been conditioned to question ourselves. To constantly look for information to validate what we are doing is right. So where do we go? Instagram! We start following all these accounts and hope someone will have the answer we need. And now because of all of this, parents are in a state of learned helplessness. We think that we can't parent or that we don't know how to parent our child.

There is no limit to the information pouring in from every corner of the internet. For us parents this is a curse more than a blessing. Every parenting Instagram account claims to have the answer to your child's issues.

Why won't my baby sleep in her crib? There is a sleep coach for that. How do I make the best organic baby food? There's a child nutritionist waiting for you with answers. You are relieved when there's a video to watch with answers. You watch the reels. Then what you really find is that there are more contradictions than answers.

There is no answer. The answer is what you believe is best for your child and your family. Your child has all the parenting information that you need.

You see at first maybe you feel like you're a smart responsible parent. You are gathering all the information, right? No matter how sound the advice may seem you're still second guessing yourself.

You're overthinking because you really care and you don't want to fail. But no amount of researching, worrying, or over analyzing can give you control over what happens next. So, loosen your grip and experience parenthood as it comes.

Early on I tried to be a gentle parent. It sounded like an amazing concept. Being empathetic and connected to your child sounded great. It didn't work for me. I tried. My child would call me out. I'd say to them "it looks like you're feeling mad" and she would yell back "YES I'M MAD". I tried many approaches I had read about. I was desperate to be the best parent and give my child the best upbringing. What I realized was that I wasn't going to find my answer unless I looked inside of me and healed myself and focused on what was important to me. I started paying attention to my child. I met them where they were at in the moment. It worked magically. We did it together and I learned there was no better way for us.

Journal Prompt Break

This may take some looking deep into your past. I want to encourage you to think of anything that seems out of the ordinary. Maybe you remember comparing your parents to your friend's parents. Think about the feelings you had. Something made you long for something different. What were those feelings? What did you wish you had instead? Take this moment to journal. Give yourself some grace. Facing our past is not always easy. Sometimes we are closed off and disconnected from our experiences to see how not normal they were. It's OK to have had experienced things differently. If we allow ourselves to work through what bothered us, we can be better parents to our children. Without those experiences we would have nothing to compare to.

I encourage you to go through the prompts and be honest and intentional with your thoughts. Write down your feelings. Do the work to get you to a place of clarity. The clarity will help guide you to how you want to parent. The choice is yours. You get to decide what's best for your child and your family.

- How do you show love to your child?
- What is the hardest part of being a parent?
- Is there a type of parent that you strive to be? What does that parenting style look like?

The Basics of Behavior

Let's talk about behavior. This is a topic I love speaking about when I do my parent workshops. It's one I consider myself a specialist in. Having worked in the field as a licensed professional for over 10 years and in my own private practice and having treated thousands of children I have earned my "knowledge badge". Understanding behavior is the single most important thing you'll need to understand with children. This is because children have lots of behaviors. It's the way they communicate when they haven't reached the necessary development needed to convey to us what they need. When we can understand behavior, we are in a better position to help them get through what they are struggling with.

When I explain child behavior to a parent, I always start with a quote I love.

"Thinking of a child as behaving badly disposes you to think of punishment. Thinking of a child as struggling to handle something difficult encourages you to help them through their distress."

Look, in my opinion there is no child who is "bad". That simply doesn't exist. There is a child who doesn't know how to functionally express their need/want and what we see is a behavior.

It is the only way a child knows how to express their frustration when they haven't learned any other way. The behavior sure does get your attention. And you give them attention. Even if it's negative attention. They don't care.

So how can we help a child who is struggling?

We have to understand the function of the behavior. Why is this behavior continuing to happen? If it's continuing to happen, something is reinforcing that behavior. No behavior would continue if it wasn't reinforced in some way. This goes for any behavior even ones we have as adults.

I get a lot of parents that say something like "Jake hits his friends for no reason at all". Let me tell you. There is a reason behind every behavior and that behavior is being reinforced which is why it continues to occur.

Look, no child wakes up in the morning thinking, today I am going to make my moms, dads, sisters, grandmas, teachers, and the list goes on, life a living hell. Nope. It just doesn't happen. So, every behavior is just a behavior. It's not anything against you. Your child is not out to get you. Remember that always. It really helped me with those epic tantrums. Take them as an opportunity to teach your child. Teach them the skills they need to get their need met instead of behaving in the way that they are. But how do we do that?

We have to take a step back and a very deep breath and then tackle the tantrum.

I love the ABC system of decoding the function of a behavior.

First, we have to understand what was the antecedent that happened right before the behavior (A). What was the behavior (B) and finally what was the consequence (C).

Antecedents can be many things. Sometime it's simple to see. Other times maybe not so much. It can be things like you asked your child to put their shoes on and that triggered a behavior because they don't want to put their shoes on. Maybe a teacher asked the class to clean up and your child didn't want to clean up what they were playing with. Maybe another child snatched something from their hand. You get the point. Something happened right before the behavior.

The behavior is what we see. The kicking, the spitting, the hitting, the biting, the name calling.

The consequence is what happens right after the behavior. Consequences don't always have to be negative. They can also be positive. What did you say to your child? Did the other peers laugh? Did you take something away? Did you talk to your child about the behavior and say something like "Stop right now, we don't behave this way. Everyone is looking at you!" Whatever it was, take note.

Now you can begin to look at each behavior and try to understand what the function is.

There are 3 main functions of behavior.

1. Attention seeking
2. Avoidant/escape behavior
3. Access to tangible

If a behavior is *attention* seeking, you want to ignore the behavior (not your child) and redirect them to what you are asking them to do.

If a behavior is *avoidant or escape* behavior, you need to follow through with what you asked of them.

If the behavior is getting or maintaining *access* to something, then you need to withhold the access and follow through with what you asked of them.

So how the hell do we know what function their behavior serves?

Sometimes it's straight forward, other times not so much. I'm going to break it down for you so you can understand.

When a child is engaging in a behavior for attention you will notice with your ABC data that the consequence that follows the behavior usually involves another person. The consequence may be a teacher lecture, other children laughing, you providing help and so on. The attention can be positive or negative it doesn't matter. In a child's eyes it's all attention.

When a child is engaging in behavior to avoid or escape something you will notice the consequence will be a time out, or a break from the task, or access to an area away from other children. They are trying to get out of doing some task you have asked of them.

When the behavior is wanting access to some tangible you will notice that the consequence involves giving access to a preferred item or activity. Maybe you said it's time to get ready for bath and your child was on an iPad. The antecedent was you saying it's time for bath. The child doesn't want to go have a bath because they are playing on their iPad. So, they start kicking you and hitting and falling to the floor and then throw their iPad across the room. You then say in your stern voice "oh no, we don't behave like this and we certainly don't throw our iPad's" and your child continues to then spit at you and hit you. You say "OK, if you stop it right now, I will give you 5 more minutes but then you have to go take a bath". And your child stops immediately and runs over to retrieve their iPad and proceeds to play their game happy as a clam. You set a timer for 5 minutes. The timer goes off and your child starts again, hitting and protesting no bath. And then they toss the iPad. What did you expect to happen? You gave into their behavior and you reinforced it by allowing them on it again. Why wouldn't any child want to keep doing this if they get what they want? Their behavior is getting them exactly what they need so it works. They will keep doing it.

In order for a child to know what is expected you must be very clear with your directions. You have to be consistent and you must follow through with what you said. What does this look like? Well, let's take an example of getting ready to leave for school. You say to your child, you have 3 minutes to finish your game and then you need to get your shoes on and get your backpack because we need to leave for school.

You set a timer for 3 minutes. The timer goes off. You say OK, time to get your shoes on and get your backpack. If your child does not comply, you say "you can do it yourself or I will help you". If they get their shoes and backpack you offer verbal praise "wow, look at you, you listened the first time!". If they do not, you say "it looks like I need to help you" and you do just that. Hand over hand you get their shoes on and get their backpack and get them to the car. There is no talking or negotiating at this point. Even if they are having that epic tantrum. In the car you don't bring any attention to any of the behaviors and you continue to school. You followed through with what you said and did not give in. Your child is now learning that you mean what you say. If you keep true to your word then they will learn that it doesn't matter what they do you will still follow through. And then the magic happens. They give up.

So, if we started following through. Started placing those boundaries and holding them firm. We would start to see a decrease in the behavior.

It's not easy. That is for sure. I know we are all tired and sometimes it's easier to just give in and let them have what they want. But the reality is you will be tired and giving in forever unless you do something about it to change it. If you don't mind the tantrums and enjoy having to negotiate then you can keep doing that. Remember we have choices. We get to decide what we want to do as parents.

I want to warn you about something. When you decide you want to do this do it intentionally. Do it knowing that you are going to stick with it 100%. If you are going to give in and play that game then your child will throw the dart because they have a 50/50 chance that they will get what they want. In order for this to be effective you have to be in it for the win.

Also, warning number 2, when you do this, you will see an increase in behaviors. You're probably going to be sending me to the moon. What is this crazy lady talking about. I want this to happen. When it does it means that it is working. How? Because your child now is thinking what I was once doing is no longer working so they are now going to try other behaviors. They might destroy things, they might start spitting at you, they might start hitting their siblings or their tantrums might become bigger than before and last longer. All is good. Trust me. You continue to hold your boundary and follow through with what you asked of them. This increase in behavior is called an extinction burst. You have to reach this level to come back down. Once a child realizes no matter what they do you will still follow through they give up. Then you have compliance.

I want to also pair this with teaching. If we don't take the time to teach our children how to get our attention, or how to functionally communicate their needs to us we can't expect them to know.

DO NOT try to do this when they are in their tantrum or having their moment. They are not listening to you in that capacity and don't care what you have to say. You are actually reinforcing the behavior when you do this. I see lots of parents trying to reason with their child mid tantrum. Stop. It doesn't work. And if it does its temporary because you made a threat and now it's become fear based. So, they comply in that moment but then continue the behavior.

Instead, when you are playing or when you're in the car driving take a moment to play through a scenario and talk about what their doll or barbie or superman could do when they are feeling this way. This is the teaching you need to do in order to expect that they react differently.

I also love positive reinforcement. As parents we tend to point out all the negative behaviors we don't like. We say things like stop running, or don't hit your brother, why are you never listening, I've asked you a million times to clean up. Sound familiar? Yep, we all are guilty of it.

I'm going to ask you to try something. Start pointing out the times your child is doing things nicely. When they clean up without you asking, when they play with their brother nicely, when they are not hitting. Point those things out to them and give them a compliment. Ignore the behaviors you want to extinguish.

If you look at a typical day and count how many times you give negative feedback vs positive feedback you will be surprised. I venture to say that it's 7 negatives to 1 positive. What I want to see is the reverse. 7 positives to 1 negative.

Why do we foucs on the negative? Because it's easy. It's what we've been conditioned to do. I'm telling you now that we need to make a conscious and intentional decision to parent differently. It can start with this one simple thing. You will be surprised how children react to this.

I also love love love to try and keep my responses in a positive light. Instead of saying things like "no, we can't go to the park today" I will say "yes, we can go to the park tomorrow because right now I have to make dinner". Starting out with a yes instead of a no will decrease the chances of a tantrum happening. You also are giving an explanation of why you can't do that now. Here's another one, "stop getting all the paint all over the table", instead say "we paint on the paper". This teaches them in the same sentence what they should be doing. Your focus isn't to shame them anymore. You are teaching now. What should they be doing. This is more likely to get you the compliance you want. I also want to note that this does not mean I don't use the word NO. Trust me, when I need to, I do. What this means is that if I know that what my child is asking me is going to trigger a tantrum I try and be proactive about it. I want my life to be easier. Less stressful.

Always remember, if you can't follow through then simply don't place the demand. If you place the demand then be prepared to follow through. If you don't your child will test that boundary every single time.

There is nothing worse than seeing your child sad and upset with themselves after a tantrum. That moment when they finally calm down and come to you for a hug is priceless. And then the question comes. I know you have all heard it.

"Mommy, do you still love me?"

My go to answer each time is, "of course I love you, I just don't love the behavior."

Journal Prompt Break

I know that was a lot. I want you to think about a few things here. Think about what behaviors trigger you the most and then I want you to think about why that might be. Is it related to your mood in that moment? Is it related to something you are carrying from your childhood?

- Are the expectations of your child too high? Too low?
- Are you a parent that follows through with what you say?
- What would an ideal child look like for you?
- What behaviors can you tolerate and what behaviors trigger you?

Parenting with Intention: Positive Vibes Only: Rule Less Play More

What is intentional parenting? I'm sure you're saying to yourself of course I'm an intentional parent because I'm certainly not doing any of this accidentally. What intentional parenting means is that you have a plan and that you prioritize your time. Time is a thief and it's a resource we can never get back. The time we get with our children is precious but limited. So, we have to plan and be intentional with what we do with it. The smallest day to day decisions we make impact our child's life and they shape the course we take. You have such limited time to instill everything you want to instill in your child. Use it wisely.

Successful habits start as lessons, turn into expectations, and ingrain as lifelong habits. If you want your child to learn these things the best thing to do is to model this behavior. If you truly believe in it, you are a walking breathing being of that thing. It comes naturally. Therefore, your child sees it. You don't have to work at it. And if you want to change then you have the permission to do so. If something isn't working for you, you can decide to change it. If you are working through childhood trauma to parent differently good for you. The version of you that shows up is what your child sees. It's what they have as guidance.

Behavior is learned. Our children are watching everything we do and say. They are little sponges soaking it all up. I know you've heard that saying and it's very true. They love to model. This is so important because if you are preaching one thing to your child but acting differently, they will see that. They will call your bullshit. Trust me. I know. I have the 9-year-old that calls me out on anything and everything. Can't catch a break. My favorite one is the cuss words. I'm the queen of cuss words and my children hear them in our home. I explain to them that these are adult words and when they know how to use them appropriately, they can, but that if they use them in the wrong place or with the wrong person there might be a consequence. As you can imagine, every time I say a cuss word I get called out.

One of my other favorite things to tell parents is that if you are escalated then you cannot deescalate an escalated child. It's not possible. You have to remove your emotions from the situation and deal with it matter of fact.

I stop and take a moment to collect myself before I act. I remind myself that I am upset in this moment and think about what I need to say and do before I do. I am aware that my children are watching me to model the appropriate behavior. I remind myself often of this.

I spend a lot of time playing. I like to teach during play. Something I always say *Play more Rule less.* What does that mean?

Play play play with your child. Let your child guide the play. Let them lead. You can insert some learning moments and role play the behavior you want to see and expect from them during this play. This way you aren't just spewing out demands and lessons you want to teach them when they are escalated. You can do it in an environment where they feel safe. Play is that place for children.

It has been researched time and time again and everything points to a child doing the most meaningful deepest form of learning during play. They reenact scenarios from their day during their play. Play encourages communication. It helps develop speech skills and listening skills. In the context of play children test out new knowledge and theories.

Use this time to teach your child what you want to instill in them so it becomes a habit.

I know it's hard to *play* as an adult. Trust me. I get it. Sitting on the floor making up things is not really an adult forte. We may be tired from all the responsibilities that we have during the day. We often may think we don't have time for this when we have 505 other things to get done that day. Some days we are in survival mode only. We've been told to use our time wisely. This is wisely. Trust me.

Magic 10. Take 10 minutes a day and play. 10 minutes of undivided attention with your phone away ready to follow the lead of your child. That's all you have to give. Whenever it works for you and your day. Your child will look forward to this special time with you. It's really magical. It takes work on our end as parents. If you're willing to put in the work, you will see a child that you might have not noticed before. My children love this time with me. But I love it even more. It's the time I get to spend one on one time with them and really see their personalities emerge. We laugh and say silly things. We fantasize about anything and everything. I take this time to instill values that I want to instill. Even my 9-year-old still loves it. Of course, it looks different as they grow. Different is OK. The thing that remains the same is the undivided time they get with you.

I like to use positive language and I believe in the power of being positive. I am thoughtful about how I say things and when I say them. The language I use will either deflect a tantrum or trigger it. I don't know about you, but I don't want to be in tantrum alert mode all day long.

When you start to be intentional with your parenting you see a shift.

I want to invite you to start becoming intentional with everything you do. Do it because it feels right to you and because it's what you want to do. Not because someone or something is telling you to do it that way. Decide what is important to you that you want to pass along to your children. How you want to spend the time you have. Make the plan. Write it down. Aim for the goals you have and ignore all the background noise. The noise will always be there. There will always be some article you read, some parent, a family member, a teacher that tries to push their parenting or their knowledge on you. You are the parent of your child. You know your child best. Do what you want to do. I'm giving you permission if you need it.

Over the years I have become unavailable for all the bullshit that exists around me. I simply choose to be available for what serves me. It doesn't mean that I don't see it or hear it or that it isn't pushed on me. It means that I know I have a choice. I can decide for myself what works. This applies to life, work, home, parenting all of it. I set boundaries for myself and my family. That includes my children. I am no longer in the business of allowing others, family or not, to influence what I do with my family. What I wish is that we would stop telling people "that's still your mom" or "that's still your sister". Toxic is toxic. I don't care if it's family or not. You are allowed to disconnect from people who put you down because you don't do it their way. Create those boundaries with them. I have had to set people straight and have made it clear I am not their doormat to walk all over. I am simply unavailable for it. End of story. No explanation needed. When you make the shift it's the most empowering feeling in the universe. This is the vibe in my house. It can be the vibe for you too if you want it to be.

Journal Prompt Break

Take the time now to journal about thing that are important to you that you want to pass along to your child. Make a plan.

- What do you wan to instill?

- How will you do that?

- How important is it to you?

- What influences might you have to let go of in order to do it the way you want?

Social Emotional Intelligence

As a child therapist, social emotional intelligence in children speaks to my soul. As a parent it's something that I incorporate in our lives not only for my children but for my husband and I. This is something that I strive to teach our children and model daily. It's my love language.

To me, a child that doesn't develop social emotional intelligence will become an adult who struggles a lifetime. An adult that becomes a people pleaser. An adult that can't think for them self and therefore is easily influenced by all the outside elements.

So, what is social emotional intelligence. In simple terms it's the process of developing self-awareness, self-control, and interpersonal skills. Also known as our mental health. Mental health is as important if not more important than our physical health. We often put our focus on our child's intellectual and physical development, and their emotional development takes the back seat. A child needs emotional stability to feel safe and happy.

Being aware, understanding, and the ability to express and manage your emotions makes for a social-emotional intelligent person. People with strong social-emotional skills are better able to cope with everyday challenges that come their way. This is all vital for a successful life. They are able to work through issues that arise and make decisions that best fit their needs. They don't rely or worry about what others will say or do.

I bet you're analyzing yourself right now. Are you socially-emotionally intelligent?

Children need the experience of feeling emotions and they need to practice tolerating their emotions to develop a sense of self-control and emotional intelligence.

I run into adults daily who haven't developed these qualities and let me tell you, it's evident and honestly ugly. Nothing worse than an adult who is so self-centered. We all know them. I personally don't want my children to grow up thinking the world owes them anything. So, in our home we preach and teach how to build social emotional intelligence.

It's really simple. Don't make it complicated.

In order to achieve social-emotional intelligence there are a few things that need to align.

First you need to acknowledge your emotions and be able to process your emotions. Then you must be able to have self-awareness on what triggers those emotions and be able to self-regulate. You must be able to control your response to your emotions. You have to be able to embrace being uncomfortable while you work through those emotions. You must learn to have empathy and accept that you are not your emotions. Finally, you must have developed social skills.

As a parent you can help foster these things in your home. Start with being aware of your child's emotions. When emotions run big, we say things we normally might not. This is what children do all the time. We can teach our children what emotions are and label them when they display those emotions. Their emotions are an opportunity to connect and teach them. Emotions are to be respected and talked through. You may want to shield them from feeling some of these big emotions but doing this will not benefit them at all. They need to feel these feelings and work through them. Listen and validate for your child. Allow them to experience these different feelings and practice tolerating them. Come up with a solution to help them problem solve. Being able to self-regulate your emotions is the biggest component of emotional intelligence. Giving them to tools to use.

Teaching your child self- control in the early years will set up the foundation for achievement. When a child is able to inhibit their impulses, they are able to engage in better behavior choices and accomplish their goals.

I hear a lot of children say things like I am sad. Or I am mad. We want to shift that language to an I feel statement. I feel sad, I feel mad. When we do this, we shift from defining ourselves to understanding that it's simply how we feel in that moment. We can then help a child figure out how to deal with that feeling without labeling them as the issue.

Children need to feel safe in order to thrive emotionally. When children feel loved they are able to explore. Make yourself available to your child. Be there for them during difficult times to help encourage them. Is your home environment a safe space for your child?

Routines help foster social emotional intelligence. Children who have daily routines feel more secure because their days are predictable. They like knowing what to expect. Routines for bathing, eating, sleeping and playing give them the structure they crave. Whatever routine you create for your family is perfect. You don't have to follow anyone's schedule. What works for you and your child is the winner.

Children not only need consistency but also discipline. This is how we teach them about acceptable behaviors. It is so important that children learn how to live respectfully. When they learn to exist in the world appropriately, self-confidence soars and their motivation grows. They need to be held accountable for their actions and learn that their actions have consequences.

Love the heck out of your children. Unconditional love is vital. Build that bond between you and your child. Feeling loved is the single most important emotional need for children. In whatever way you show your love, do it often and consistently.

Teach your child gratitude. Gratitude is such an important quality that I feel many parents have put to the side. I see way less children who are grateful and express appreciation. Even simple manners like *please* and *thank you* are non-existent in the generation of children now. How did we get away from these simple things? Listen, the world doesn't owe your child anything. Children must be taught gratitude and it starts with how you as the parent model it and talk about it in your home. It can be as simple as sharing something everyone is grateful for while you're eating dinner. I make it a practice to talk about what we are grateful for in our home. Sometimes it's at dinner, other times it's when we are all in the car. Doesn't matter when or where but it gets done. I am not raising children who are ungrateful. Period. I put a roof over their head, I feed them, and give them everything they need. They will learn to be grateful. More often than not we blame the child but really the fault is with us. We baby our children, and spoil them rotten and they expect this. But this is not reality. So we have to stop.

Allow your child to be their own person. They are unique and you want to allow them to reach their full potential. Let them become their own person as you guide them to find that person. In a safe, relaxed, loving environment they will be able to develop their own personality.

Our current world has been focused so much on education and academic achievement in early childhood years that emotional self-regulation has been ignored. If you ask me, we are making a huge mistake and we are starting to see the damage of this practice.

What happened to children playing and being children. Why are we pushing academics at such young ages. And the age gets younger and younger as we go.

When I was growing up, parents didn't feel the pressure to have their toddlers be little baby geniuses at 2. Parents weren't trying to teach their children letters and numbers or how to write their name. Children were out riding bikes, playing in the dirty, jumping in puddles and creating elaborate forts. Parents weren't asking each other if their child could count or read. Now, that is at the top of every conversation I hear. What preschool is your child going to attend? Do they focus on academics? What learning model do they use? I cringe every time. None of my children went to preschool. I kept them home. We went to the park. They socialized with other children. They learned conflict resolution. They learned teamwork. We spent our days painting, planting, exploring and playing.

I'm here to tell you that it's OK if your child doesn't know their ABC's or can count or write their name when they start school. They have a lifetime of schooling to learn all that. They will learn it. Trust me. Spend the younger years working on social emotional intelligence instead. You'll thank me later.

Give them the skills. Model the skills. Teach the skills.

Journal Prompt Break

I want you to think back to your childhood. Think about what was expected of you. I want you to think about what expectations you have for your child now. Is it different or the same?

- Do you have social emotional intelligence?
- Is social emotional intelligence important to you and your family? If it is, how do you or will you incorporate it into your family?
- If you chose social emotional intelligence, does it mean that you don't value education?

Getting Back to the Basics

Social media has become both a blessing and a curse for parents. It's a place where we can find our village and have a sense of community and a place to share our biggest achievements and our worries. It's also a place where we can get support or even bashed. It's a place with way too much information and advice that has created a parenting nightmare for many.

We have to change this. It starts with you and your family. With you making an intentional decision to want to parent in a way that works for you and your child.

Create your own parenting style. The one where you get to raise your child the way you want. In the way that your child needs. Without all the background noise that's making you do things that don't feel right.

Start with family time. Get to know your child. Their needs. Their personality. One way to do this is to spend time with them. Spend time as a family. We have lost sight of this practice. Many of us don't even eat together anymore. We have families with two working parents, parents who work late, families where sports and activities have taken over that we rush home and throw down food for our kids and rush them to eat and get in the bath and to bed. We are a society where we are going nonstop. You can sit there and make excuses all day long for why you don't have time to eat dinner together or play a game or take the walk. Or you can make a change. If you work late and family dinner can't happen, then it can be morning family breakfast. Whatever it is, I don't care and your child doesn't either. If this is something you want you will find a way to make it work. The excuse is just a mask that you use as a shield. I implore you to think about what is important and get back to spending some time with your family. If it's weekly or daily it doesn't matter. Just make the time.

Family time is so important in our home. We value it more than scheduled activities. Why? Because weekends spent collecting rocks and treasures, going to the beach and looking for shells, or riding bikes with our kids are the moments that really matter. A busy schedule of sports and activities was only starving our family time and getting in the way of nurturing our family relationships. We love our family lunch time. It's the time that works for all of us most days. So, we go with it. We enjoy family vacations, even if they are day trips. We pack the car and head out for the day. I can't tell you the happiness and joy that radiates from each of our children. Activities happen in our home but they are limited to one thing per child. Sometimes it's dance, or gymnastics other times it's karate or swimming. Some months it's nothing at all and that's fine too.

I see families where every day has some sport or activity and the parents are going from one place to another. Zero time spent with the child. Children don't need to be engaged every second of the day. Downtime is actually critical. Children need to learn to entertain themselves.

We are creating this world where we think we need to keep children busy all the time. We don't. I don't care what social media is telling you or what your mom friends are doing. You don't have to do it if it doesn't fit what you want your parenting life to look like. Get back to the basics.

Spending one on one time with my children by having a date day also happens in our home. This is a monthly thing. They each get to pick where and what we do. I can't tell you how much I value this time with each of them. And I know they need it. Such a small simple thing but so important. I want them to feel seen, to feel heard, to get to do something with me where they have my undivided attention. Sometimes we get dressed up and go all out if that's what they want. Other times we throw our hair up and go shopping all day. Whatever it is, I'm in it for the time I get to spend with them. The stories we share, the uncontrollable laughter, the smiles, it's all magical. For both of us.

We need to get back to boundary setting. It's OK and children need to know that you are in charge of their well-being. That you make the rules. That there are rules and things that they have to comply with. When did we get away from this? Why? I honestly don't have the answer, but what I do know is that now, more than ever, we have children who think that rules don't apply to them. That teachers, and other adults can't tell them what to do. This is very scary. Very very scary. Children are talking back to their teachers. They are in school behaving in ways that are completely inappropriate. They are bullying other children. Schools are struggling on how to deal with this. The parents of these children are at the principal's office trying to make excuses for their child's behaviors. Trying to validate why it's ok for their child to be acting this way and even worse trying to tell school staff how they can and can't deal with it. And school administrators are all walking on eggshells around these parents. It all has to stop.

I have news for you, these children will have a tough tough time out in the real world. What happened to raising a child with tough skin? Children today don't even know what this means. I will say it again, the world is not a gentle world. Children need to learn to cope and deal with the real world. When they go get a job and their employer doesn't put up with their nonsense then what? I'll tell you what, they quit. They go from job to job with the same issues following them. We must get back to having some authority as parents. You are not your child's best friend. You are their parent. Start parenting. Children have zero conflict resolution skills. They will grow up to be self-entitled brats. There is no resolution for them because they have been catered by bullshit their whole life The complex that they have is unreal.

Yes, we want children to learn to be independent. To build their confidence skills. To have choices. To be able to stand up for themselves. Yes. Agreed 100%. But, there's always a but. We also need them to have respect for authority. They need to understand that there are rules and things we must do even if we don't like the rule. That there are consequences in life. That we always have a choice but we must be willing to accept the consequence at times if that's the choice we make. That's the difference.

Children can't be living in a world shielded because we think we need to protect them from hearing the word "NO" because if we use that word, we will be damaging them when we set boundaries.

There's a balance for everything. We can't always be the good, positive, do it all parent. We need to help our children grow and learn. We have to enforce rules. Set boundaries. Follow through. We need to find that balance. It's our job. Remember it might look different from child to child. That's OK. You must be willing to adapt and change as you parent each child.

If this resonates with you and you are hearing what I am saying you have the ability to make a change now. It doesn't matter what age your child is. It's never too late. You can start now and give your child the best gift. The gift of becoming a productive functioning member of society.

Journal Prompt Break

You are rocking this. I'm sure by now you have thought more about your parenting and your child than you have ever in the past.

- If you could start over in your parenting journey, what would you do differently? Can you start that now and make a difference?
- What or who inspires you to be a better parent? Why?
- Are the expectations for you as a parent too high?
- What do you want your legacy to be?

Self-Care Like No Other- It's The Vibe Around Here

Self-Care has been thrown around for the last few years and has become a catchphrase that people often associate with over the top, luxurious pleasures. Parents get triggered when people tell them to take a nap when the baby is napping or go shopping. It's triggering because in their mind they don't even have enough time in a day to take care of the basic necessities. Where parents fail is that they don't perceive self-care as a necessity. Rather it's a luxury. We need to change this. Self- care doesn't need to be over the top. It can be simple, a few minutes a day to rejuvenate doing something that fills your soul. Whatever that is for you.

Parents struggle with making time for themselves, and it's especially difficult for new parents. The biggest reason is because self-care changes as you enter this new stage of your life. The things that fed your soul before may be different now. And that's OK. Learning what the new you needs may take time. Be gentle with yourself. Allow yourself to accept where you are now and more importantly accept that things may look different.

Sometimes a small daily self-care act is perfect. Other days you need a couple hours to yourself. Maybe you need a day or several days. It's all OK and all acceptable. It can all be fluid and allowed to change whenever you feel compelled to do so. From person to person, situation to situation self-care can be whatever makes your soul feel alive. It can be as simple as putting on nice clothes. It can be taking a hot bubble bath. A dinner with your best friend or a night at a hotel with your favorite book. Whatever it is, you are allowed. Often times when we are in the thick of parenting and we feel like we have no time to do the day-to-day things let alone take time for ourselves. If you are in a place where you are feeling like that, then self-care can look like you asking for someone to come watch your child so that you can eat a hot meal. Maybe you want sleep. Hire that sitter and go sleep for 3 hours. You are allowed. You should. Make yourself a priority.

I get asked a lot what does my self care look like? For me it's a must daily. Even if it's only 10 minutes. It happens. There is no negotiating on that. Most nights I make it a point to get in bed by 930 after I've put the kids to bed. Yes, it sounds like a dream to some of you and it once was a dream for me but I couldn't hang like I did in my 20's. I like to spend some time scrolling mindlessly through my phone on Pinterest, Instagram surfing or watching mindless TV. No mom duties, no house duties, no husband duties and no to do lists. This is often the only time I get all day to myself to just do me. I am intentional about it. The never-ending list of things I need to do will always be there. The thoughts come into my head and if I allow them, they consume me. So, I don't. I've learned that tomorrow is a perfect time to tackle those things. I tell myself, today, right now, I am doing me. I feel no guilt. No shame. I know I need this time to decompress so that I can be the best version of myself. For my own sanity.

Self- care is so important to my mental health that I participate in the "parking lot self-care". If you know, you know. If you have never heard of this, let me let you in on a little secret. Drive to a store and park your car. Sit and listen to music, indulge in the snacks, or any other mindless activity you want. It can be this small. But, wow, what a gift to yourself. The quiet time, no child calling "mommy" 505 times. No disruptions. It's magical. A vibe that I'm here for. It doesn't have to be anything over the top. Self-care only needs to serve you in the way you want it to.

Other things I do that make me feel human and require some more planning. They are also important to me. I go on girl trips with my friends. Sometimes its over night and sometimes it's day trips. I love getting my hair and nails done and a good massage is prioritized. Going shopping alone is always available to me. Solo lunch dates are often the vibe and happen weekly. Solo trips are also a vibe for me. I go and get a hotel room and fully enjoy. It's intentional. It's what I make a priority along with other things I deem important. I insert time into my schedule to do all these things. See the thing is if you don't schedule the time, it likely won't happen. You'll keep putting it off and before you know it it's been months. Think of it as something you need not want. I need a break. I need time to myself. I need to re-energize. Make it happen.

There was a period of time in my life early on in my parenting journey where I would feel shame and guilt around carving out time to myself. Society and the background noise talking about the perfect mom who does it all was what I thought I needed to be. Now, in this period of my parenthood journey I am unavailable for anything that doesn't serve me. You can be too. It's all up to you and what you chose to allow and not allow. Our brains are powerful beasts. If we allow them to be consumed by nonsense that doesn't serve us or our family or our child then that's on us. But we have a choice. A choice to intentionally decide what things will look like for us. What is OK and acceptable. Without any judgment. Without worrying about what anyone will say.

So, take care of yourself. First. Just like on the airplane when they tell you to put on your oxygen mask before you help your child or another person. You know what I'm talking about because it feels like everything we hear or read brings mention to this. But if you don't help your child first then you're being selfish and only thinking about yourself, right? No. I don't allow those thoughts. For me it's more like, I must take care of myself because I am worthy of it. It's not an option for me. Or a choice. It's a must. Without my time and my space daily, I would lose my ever-loving mind. Yes, I also wouldn't be able to be fully present for my children, but that's not the sole reason why I chose me. Self-care is about me.

Ask yourself, are you worthy of your own time? Your own love? The answer is yes. Proclaim that to the world. Taking care of yourself is the hardest job. It's so much easier to take care of others. I get it. But make the time. Your mental health needs it.

Not because your child needs it. Not because your spouse wants you to. Not because society is telling you to.

But because *you* want to. Because it makes *you* feel good. Because *you* love loving on yourself.

And if your child benefits, then double win.

It's also important to me that my children see that this is OK. That it's OK to take care of yourself. To make yourself a priority. To do things you like. Because I exist outside of my parent role. I have a life too. I love myself enough to be OK with doing things that make me happy even if it doesn't include them all the time. I want them to also know they exist outside of me.

We talk about the importance of self-care in our home. My girls are queens of self-care. They love their bubble baths, their time alone in their rooms, doing their hair and makeup and nails. We talk about wanting some space and having alone time. Alone time is a form of self-care. I tell them that it is absolutely acceptable to ask for time to take care of themselves. When any of my children ask for time to love on themselves, I happily give it to them. It's all important. In whatever way it looks for them in that moment in their life. When you make it important your children see it.

You know what's funny? Anytime I go out without my kids, someone always asks as if it is a crime that they aren't attached to my hip. How dare I leave them at home so that I can enjoy some time to myself. What kind of mother am I that I would do such a thing? Let me tell you the kind.... The kind that makes herself a priority and wants to keep her sanity.

I have zero guilt when I go out. Why? Because I know I need it. I need to feel human and have adult connections. I talk to my children about this. Openly. No shame. There was a time in my life where I did feel ashamed. Where I wouldn't go out because I was brainwashed into the societal bullshit. Heck, even my own mother starts with her "again you're out. Don't you have a husband and children to take care of?" whenever she calls me and I tell her I'm out. I am a grown ass adult, yet still the generational beliefs are real and very alive. Even so, I still carry on my life. I don't allow it to influence me in any way. In fact, the opposite happens. I cringe every time my mother tells me these things and usually fire back some smart comment like "yes, my husband is a capable adult and my children are just fine". And I carry on. Zero shame.

If you need a little jump start on how to prioritize yourself, I want you to think about these three questions. What matters the most to you? How do you want to be remembered? What is best for you?

These questions remind me that my time is limited, the time I have is precious to me and life is too short to neglect yourself. I chose not to go through the motions on overload and exhaustion day in and day out. I decide what is worth me doing and what is not. I learned a long time ago to say "No" to things that only add stress to my life. I don't need to be a super parent. I don't need to gain anyone's approval. I don't need validation. I give it to myself. Time and time again. Every single day. This has allowed me to have time for myself. Instead of giving all my time to everyone else, I learned saying "no" is OK. Those that respect you will respect your "no". This doesn't mean that I don't do a lot of things. I actually am beyond involved on so many levels with so many things.

Because I want to be and I make it work in my day. I know my limits. I know what I can handle. When my plate starts to get too full, I know how to say "no".

* * *

I leave you with this......

Parenting never stops until the day you're called to heaven. You'll stay up late when everyone has gone to sleep planning your next day. You'll wake up early while everyone is still sleeping to get a jump start on the day. You'll sleep with an ear still listening and an eye still open for someone to call out your name. You'll look ahead, yet always reminisce. Always aware of how little time you have. No matter how old your children are you always will want them to come to you when the world feels big and heavy. You will always be waiting and available. That's what you do. I see you and I know this is the hardest job you'll ever have. You've got this.

Journal Prompt Break

You made it. You read this book and did the work. I am so proud of you. I want to know what has changed for you or what you're going to work on changing as you move through this parenting journey in life after reading this book. If you have any feelings towards allowing time for yourself, I want you to break down those feelings and allow yourself the space to work through why those feelings are there.

You are allowed to have time to yourself daily. Nobody gets to tell you that you don't or make you feel ashamed or less than if you do. We are letting go of those thoughts. Shift to a place where you do things that serve you and your family. Taking care of yourself can be one of those things.

- Do you take time for yourself? What does that time look like for you?
- Do you want to start doing something differently when you give yourself some self-care time? What will that look like for you
- Who can you lean on for support?

About the Author

A mom, wife, daughter, sister, child therapist and boss lady. She was born and raised in beautiful Santa Monica, California. Currently living in Ventura County with her family. A Cali girl through and through! Georgia has 3 daughters that are her whole world. She has been working with children her entire life and naturally becoming a child therapist was in the cards. When she isn't running her own private practice and business, she enjoys going to the beach and photography. Vacationing with her family is top priority. Family time is a vibe and sacred in her home. She loves to teach and speak about childhood disorders, behaviors and social emotional intelligence in children. Her passion radiates through her work. If you're lucky enough to meet her in person at a workshop or sit in live on any of her recordings you will experience the magic that she brings.

https://thebehaviorboss.com